FREEDOM'S
PROMISE

RUBY BRIDGES
AND THE DESEGREGATION
OF AMERICAN SCHOOLS

D1117780

BY DUCHESS HARRIS, JD, PHD

WITH TOM HEAD

Core Library

An Imprint of Abdo Publishing
abdobooks.com

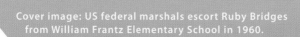
Cover image: US federal marshals escort Ruby Bridges
from William Frantz Elementary School in 1960.

abdocorelibrary.com

Published by Abdo Publishing, a division of ABDO, PO Box 398166, Minneapolis, Minnesota 55439. Copyright © 2019 by Abdo Consulting Group, Inc. International copyrights reserved in all countries. No part of this book may be reproduced in any form without written permission from the publisher. Core Library™ is a trademark and logo of Abdo Publishing.

Printed in the United States of America, North Mankato, Minnesota
092018
012019

THIS BOOK CONTAINS RECYCLED MATERIALS

Cover Photo: AP Images
Interior Photos: AP Images, 1; Pete Souza/PSG/Newscom, 5; Bettmann/Getty Images, 6–7, 28, 43; Marjory Collins/Everett Collection/Newscom, 9; Everett Collection/Newscom, 12–13; Horace Cort/AP Images, 14; Everett Historical/Shutterstock Images, 17, 23; CSU Archives/Everett Collection/Newscom, 20–21; Red Line Editorial, 25, 39; Underwood Archives/UIG Universal Images Group/Newscom, 30–31; Steven Senne/AP Images, 36–37

Editor: Maddie Spalding
Series Designer: Claire Vanden Branden

Library of Congress Control Number: 2018949711

Publisher's Cataloging-in-Publication Data

Names: Harris, Duchess, author. | Head, Tom, author.
Title: Ruby Bridges and the desegregation of American schools / by Duchess
     Harris and Tom Head.
Description: Minneapolis, Minnesota : Abdo Publishing, 2019 | Series: Freedom's
     promise | Includes online resources and index.
Identifiers: ISBN 9781532117749 (lib. bdg.) | ISBN 9781641856089 (pbk) | ISBN 9781532170607
     (ebook)
Subjects: LCSH: Bridges, Ruby--Juvenile literature. | Civil rights activists--
     Juvenile literature. | School integration--United States--Juvenile literature. |
     Desegregation--Juvenile literature.
Classification: DDC 379.263--dc23

CONTENTS

A LETTER FROM DUCHESS

Artist Norman Rockwell was famous for his paintings of American life. He showed the lives of American families and American values. Sometimes he also showed America's serious problems. Rockwell did this in a painting called *The Problem We All Live With*.

His painting shows a young black girl walking to school. She wears a white dress and carries her schoolbooks. In front of her are two US marshals in suits. The scene is from a child's point of view, so the men's heads are blocked by the top of the frame. Behind the girl on a wall are a thrown tomato and a racial insult.

Who is the little girl? Her name is Ruby Bridges. She played an important role in desegregating American schools in the 1960s. Bridges faced severe hardships as she struggled to get an education. Her legacy remains strong today as an example of strength in the face of injustice.

Please join me on this journey to learn about Bridges's life and legacy, an important story of the promise of freedom.

Duchess Harris

Ruby Bridges, *left*, speaks with President Barack Obama in front of Norman Rockwell's painting *The Problem We All Live With*.

ONE

RUBY'S
FIRST DAY

On the morning of November 14, 1960, six-year-old Ruby Bridges walked up the steps to William Frantz Elementary School in New Orleans, Louisiana. Her mother walked beside her. It was Ruby's first day at the school. An angry mob shouted at her. Four US federal marshals surrounded and protected her.

Ruby did not understand why a mob of people was gathered around the school. The only thing her parents had told her was that she would be going to a new school and that she had better behave. No one had

A crowd of white protesters gathered outside William Frantz Elementary School on Ruby Bridges's first day at the school in 1960.

told her that she would be the only black student at the school.

When Ruby had first arrived at the school, she thought the mob was part of a parade. Ruby had seen people celebrate the famous Mardi Gras parade in New Orleans. They would gather in the middle of the street. They would shout and wave their hands. To Ruby, the mob of people at first looked like they were celebrating Mardi Gras.

The crowd shouted insults at Ruby. But Ruby only became scared when she

PERSPECTIVES
BARBARA HENRY

Barbara Henry was Ruby's only first-grade teacher at William Frantz Elementary School. All other teachers at the school refused to teach Ruby. Each day Ruby sat in a classroom by herself. Henry taught her in every subject, including physical education and music. In a later interview, Henry remembered, "We created our own oasis of love and learning. We each had hearts free of prejudice. That was the bond that united us." Henry and Ruby remained friends later in life.

In the 1960s and earlier, black children had to attend separate schools from white children.

passed a woman holding a black doll. The doll was inside a coffin. The image later gave her nightmares. She dreamed that the coffin had wings and flew around her bed at night.

Ruby was rushed inside the building. Many people in the crowd flooded in behind her. Ruby and her mother took refuge inside the principal's office. Ruby watched through the office's windows as people pointed and shouted at her. Parents took their children out of the school. Ruby did not know why they were angry. She only knew that she had not been prepared for this.

WHEN READING WAS ILLEGAL

Slaveholders did not want enslaved people to read. Slaveholders thought enslaved people would rebel if they knew how to read. Southern states made it illegal for enslaved people to learn how to read. Anyone who taught an enslaved person to read could be fined, jailed, or whipped.

THE RIGHT TO AN EDUCATION

In the 1960s, most schools were racially segregated in the South. Black and white children had to attend separate schools. Often the schools and resources provided for black children were not as good as those provided for white children. This unequal treatment had been going on for many years.

Before the American Civil War (1861–1865), enslaved people were not allowed to attend school. At the end of the war, the US government changed this rule. It required southern states that had seceded during the war to teach both white and black children. If they did not, these states would not be allowed to rejoin the United States. But schools were not required to teach black and white children together in the same classrooms. Many white teachers refused to teach black students. Schools became racially segregated. School integration, or the enrollment of black children in all-white schools, was meant to change this. School integration in the South began in the 1950s. Ruby was one of the first black children to integrate a white elementary school in the South.

EXPLORE ONLINE

Chapter One talks about Ruby Bridges's first day at William Frantz Elementary. The website below goes into more depth on this topic. As you know, every source is different. What information does the website give about this topic? How is the information from the website the same as the information in Chapter One? What new information did you learn?

RUBY BRIDGES GOES TO SCHOOL
abdocorelibrary.com/ruby-bridges

CHAPTER
TWO

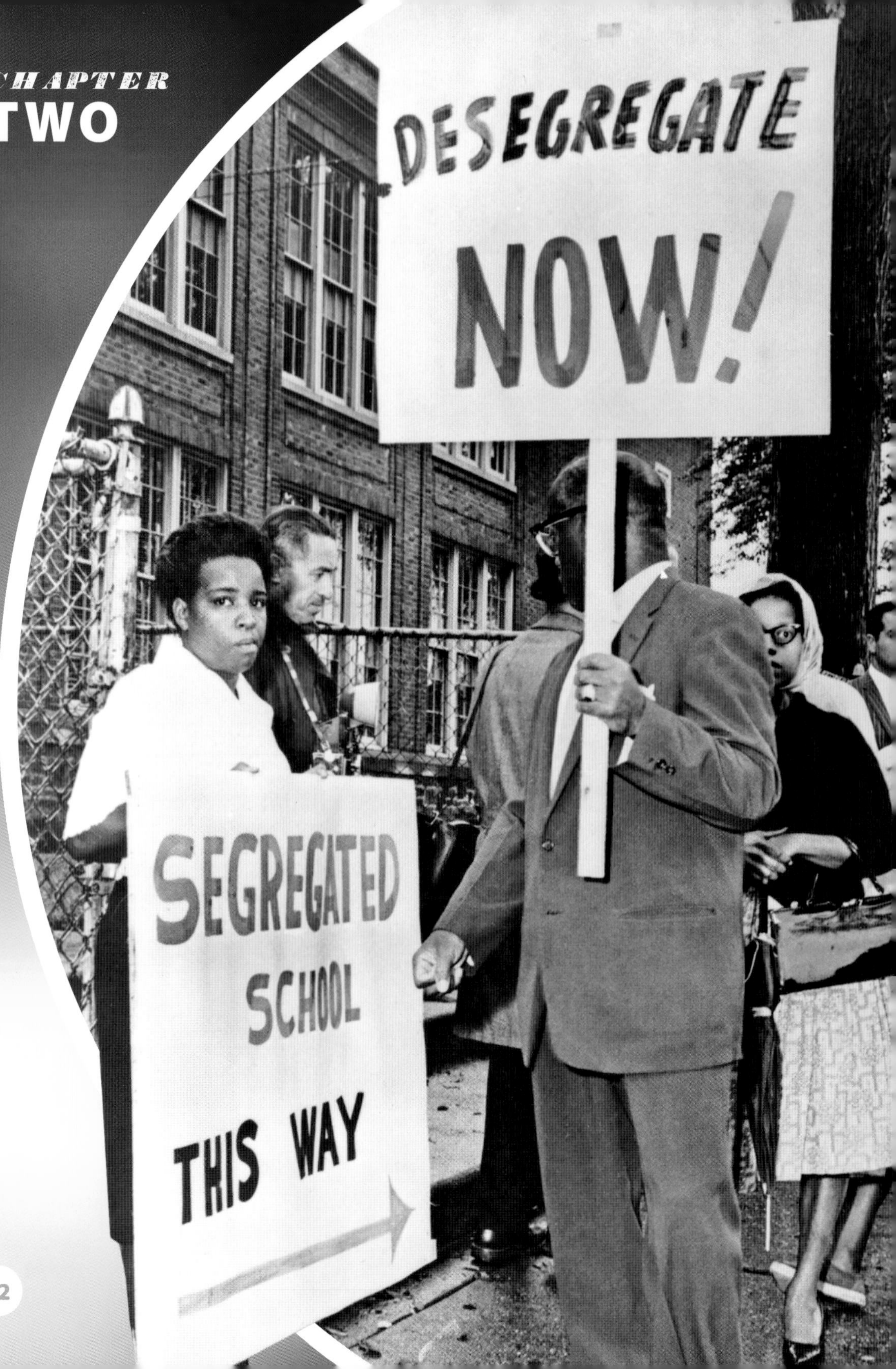

THE ROAD TO *BROWN*

School segregation was part of a larger problem in the South. Throughout the late 1800s and most of the 1900s, African Americans were segregated in many ways in the South. The Fourteenth Amendment had been passed in 1868. This amendment to the US Constitution says that every citizen should be given equal rights and protection under the law. These rights include equal access to education. But southern leaders disagreed. They wanted to make sure black people did not have the same rights as white people. Beginning in the late 1870s, they passed a series of laws called Jim Crow laws.

A group of activists protests school segregation in 1962.

13

In the Jim Crow South, African American passengers were required to sit at the back of buses.

These laws enforced racial segregation. Black and white people were separated in public places, such as parks and theaters. Black people had to use separate facilities, such as drinking fountains. They could not attend the same schools as white people.

In 1892 a black man named Homer Plessy boarded a whites-only train car. He refused to move. He was arrested. He argued that separating people by race in train cars violated the Fourteenth Amendment. His case went up to the US Supreme Court.

In 1896 the Supreme Court ruled in *Plessy v. Ferguson.* The court said segregation was legal as long as white and black people were treated equally. Southern states continued to segregate people by race. They did not treat black and white people equally.

BLACK ACTIVISM

In the 1900s, black activists such as W. E. B. Du Bois fought to end segregation. Du Bois was one of the founders of the National Association for the Advancement of Colored People (NAACP). This group's goal is to improve the lives of African Americans. Du Bois focused on the fight for equality and better civil rights laws. Other black activists, such as Booker T. Washington, believed that black communities needed to help themselves before desegregation could happen. Washington said that black people needed to focus on education and learning new skills to build their careers. He argued that this would make white people respect black people more. Then he believed white people would accept black people as equal citizens. In these ways, Du Bois and Washington developed different strategies for fighting discrimination. But both forms of activism were important during the civil rights movement.

Washington's method helped improve education and expand the school system in black communities. Washington founded Tuskegee University in Alabama. This school taught black students at a time when most schools would not accept them. Du Bois's method helped end segregation. Important court cases in the

Booker T. Washington, who was formerly enslaved, promoted education in black communities.

mid-1900s would lead to desegregation efforts around the country.

In 1938 the US Supreme Court ruled that states must allow black students to get a full education. This meant that black students could attend white schools that had programs not offered by black schools. This ruling allowed black students to go to law school

In 1948 President Harry Truman issued Executive Order 9981. This order ended segregation in the US military. This turned white southerners against Truman. It also showed the country that ending segregation was possible. This gave some activists hope that desegregation could happen soon in other areas.

and medical school. In 1940 a federal court said that black and white teachers who taught in the same school district must be paid the same salary. In 1947 another federal court ruled that California schools could not separate white and Latino students. Then the Supreme Court made a landmark decision in 1954. NAACP lawyer Thurgood Marshall argued in a case called *Brown v. Board of Education of Topeka*. Marshall said segregation taught black children that they were inferior to white children. He said these ideas were harmful to black children. The court agreed with him. It said that school segregation violated the Fourteenth Amendment. The court ruling required states to begin desegregating public schools.

STRAIGHT TO THE
SOURCE

Chief Justice Earl Warren gave the court's reasons for the
***Brown v. Board of Education* ruling in 1954:**

Today, education is perhaps the most important function of state and local governments. . . . It is doubtful that any child may reasonably be expected to succeed in life if he is denied the opportunity of an education. Such an opportunity, where the state has undertaken to provide it, is a right which must be made available to all on equal terms. . . .

To separate [black children] from others of similar age and qualifications solely because of their race generates a feeling of inferiority as to their status in the community that may affect their hearts and minds in a way unlikely ever to be undone.

Source: "Brown v. Board of Education." *Legal Information Institute*. Cornell, 1954. Web. Accessed August 10, 2018.

Consider Your Audience

Adapt this passage for a different audience, such as your principal or friends. Write a blog post conveying this same information for the new audience. How does your post differ from the original text and why?

SCHOOL DESEGREGATION

The *Brown* ruling did not immediately end segregation. Most white southerners opposed the ruling. Approximately 100 southern politicians signed a letter in March 1956. This letter was called the "Southern Manifesto." In it, the politicians promised to resist integration.

Some white people used violence to fight desegregation. A group of white southerners formed an organization called the Ku Klux Klan (KKK) in 1866. In the 1950s and 1960s, the KKK damaged or destroyed hundreds of black churches and schools throughout the South.

Firefighters in Birmingham, Alabama, spray African American protesters with high-pressure water from a fire hose in 1963.

21

THE CITIZENS' COUNCILS

Groups called Citizens' Councils formed after the *Brown* decision. They wanted schools to remain segregated. White employers and police officers often supported Citizens' Councils. They helped the groups get civil rights activists arrested or fired. Citizens' Councils also raised funds for whites-only private schools. They worked to pass new segregation laws. They worked closely with the Mississippi State Sovereignty Commission. This commission was a state-funded spy program. It spied on and harassed civil rights activists.

They killed many civil rights activists. Southern police often helped the KKK commit violence. White people hoped this violence would intimidate activists and end desegregation efforts.

Some white politicians used KKK violence as an excuse not to enforce the *Brown* ruling. They thought the KKK would become more violent once the school desegregation process began. In September 1958, the Supreme Court ruled that this was not a valid excuse. Violence or no violence, *Brown* was the law of the land.

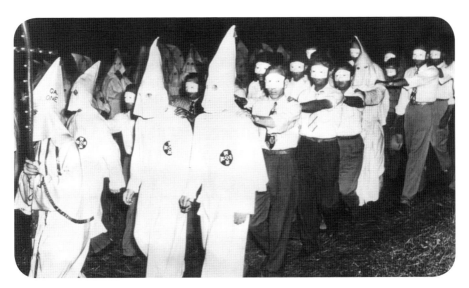

Members of the KKK sought to intimidate black people who wanted to end discrimination.

INTEGRATION

The NAACP talked to black parents about the integration process. They asked parents if they would be interested in having their children integrate schools. White schools had better resources than black schools, so integration could give black students more opportunities. But it was not an easy choice to make. Black students who attempted to integrate faced the threat of violence. This threat extended to their families. There was also no guarantee that the integration attempt would be successful.

In 1957 the NAACP found nine black teenagers who were willing integrate Little Rock Central High School in Little Rock, Arkansas. But when the students tried to attend classes on September 4, the Arkansas National Guard stopped them from entering the school. The governor of Arkansas had summoned the guardsmen. On September 25, President Dwight Eisenhower put the US government in control of the Arkansas National Guard. He told the guardsmen to escort the students into the school. This time their integration attempt was successful.

RUBY MAKES HISTORY

Ruby Bridges was born in September 1954, about four months after the *Brown* decision. Ruby grew up on a farm in Mississippi. Her parents decided to move to New Orleans when Ruby was four years old. They hoped to find more employment opportunities in the city. Ruby's father found work at a gas station. Her mother took odd jobs to support the family.

SCHOOL DESEGREGATION TIMELINE

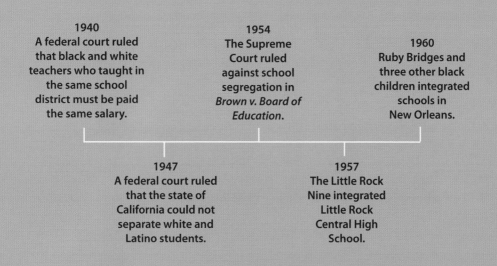

1940
A federal court ruled that black and white teachers who taught in the same school district must be paid the same salary.

1954
The Supreme Court ruled against school segregation in *Brown v. Board of Education*.

1960
Ruby Bridges and three other black children integrated schools in New Orleans.

1947
A federal court ruled that the state of California could not separate white and Latino students.

1957
The Little Rock Nine integrated Little Rock Central High School.

The above timeline shows some key events that occurred before and during the period of school desegregation in the South. How did these events pave the way for desegregation efforts?

It took six years for school desegregation to begin in New Orleans. By then Ruby was old enough to attend school. Ruby's school district required black students who wanted to attend white schools to take an entrance exam. The exam measured their academic abilities. Ruby and five other students passed the exam. Two of the students decided to remain in black schools.

Three other students integrated McDonough Elementary School. William Frantz Elementary School was the closest elementary school to the Bridges' home. Ruby would be the only black student to integrate at the school. Ruby and the three other children would be the first black students to integrate white public elementary schools in the South.

Ruby's father worried about Ruby's safety. He did not at

first want Ruby to enroll at William Frantz Elementary. But Ruby's mother persuaded him to let Ruby attend the school. She wanted Ruby to have a good education. A federal judge asked the US government to send federal marshals to protect Ruby and the other African American children. Ruby's mother also accompanied Ruby during her first few days at the new school.

Ruby had a hard first year at William Frantz Elementary. She often felt lonely. She usually ate lunch alone. Other students did not interact with her. Protesters came to the school each day. One woman threatened to poison Ruby's food. After this threat, Ruby was only allowed to eat food prepared at her home.

Ruby's parents faced discrimination after they enrolled Ruby at William Frantz Elementary. Customers threatened to boycott the gas station where Ruby's father worked. Ruby's father was fired from his job. The owner of the neighborhood grocery store did not allow

Ruby's parents to shop there. But many people stepped in to help the Bridges. A neighbor gave Ruby's father a job painting houses. Other neighbors helped take care of Ruby and her siblings. People across the country had heard Ruby's story. Many people sent the Bridges gifts, money, and letters of support.

Over time, parents began bringing their children back to William Frantz Elementary. Some of the white children came back. The mob outside the school became smaller throughout the school year. By the time Ruby entered second grade, protesters no longer gathered outside the school. Other black students also began to attend the school. Ruby was finally taught in a classroom with other students.

Ruby was supported at home but had a difficult first year at William Frantz Elementary.

OBSTACLES TO DESEGREGATION

By the late 1960s, many schools across the country had desegregated. In 1968 nearly one in four black students went to majority-white schools. But there still were obstacles to desegregation. Many neighborhoods were segregated. Black and white people often lived in separate areas. Many black people did not live near majority-white schools.

In 1969 a federal judge ordered a school district in North Carolina to begin a busing program. Busing involves transporting students by bus to schools outside of their local school districts. Many majority-white schools were

School desegregation happened gradually across the South in the 1950s and 1960s.

in suburban areas. Many majority-black schools were in cities. Black students were bused every day to majority-white schools. White students were bused to majority-black schools. Soon other school districts across the country also began busing programs.

WHITE FLIGHT

Busing was meant to speed up the school desegregation process. School districts hoped it would help the number of white and black students in schools become more equal. But many white people protested busing. Some white students refused to take part in busing programs. Parents of white students thought the neighborhoods their children were bused to were unsafe.

Busing programs ended in many cities because of widespread opposition. Many wealthy white people also moved out of areas that had busing programs. They settled in suburban areas. This movement is called white flight.

Schools are often supported by property taxes. Wealthy families often own a lot of property and pay higher property taxes. When wealthy white people moved from cities to suburbs, city schools lost funding. Many city public schools today teach black and minority students. These schools receive less funding than private, suburban schools. They are frequently overcrowded.

White flight continues today. This trend has made schools more segregated today than they were in the

VOUCHERS

In 1959 officials in Prince Edward County, Virginia, shut down public schools instead of integrating them. Students were given coupons called vouchers to attend new private schools. These schools only allowed white students to enroll. In 1964 the Supreme Court ruled that replacing public schools with whites-only private schools violated *Brown*. But the voucher system is still in place today. Vouchers often only cover part of a private school's cost. Families have to cover the rest of the cost. White families tend to be wealthier than black families. In this way, the voucher system keeps many black students from attending private schools.

late 1960s. By 1998 fewer than one in three black students went to mostly white schools. By 2011 fewer than one in four did.

DESEGREGATION EFFORTS

Activists today consider actions that may help desegregate schools. One possible solution is magnet schools. Magnet schools are public schools that offer specialized classes, such as world languages. These specialized programs may help bring more white students into communities of color. Some school districts have also redrawn zoning lines. Zoning lines decide the communities that are within a certain school district. Redrawing these boundaries could change the makeup of school districts. Then the districts could include both white communities and communities of color. These actions could help desegregate schools in the future.

FURTHER EVIDENCE

Chapter Four explores desegregation efforts such as busing programs. What was one of the main points of this chapter? What evidence is included to support this point? Read the article at the website below. Does the information on the website support the main point of the chapter? Does it present new evidence?

BUS TO THE BURBS
abdocorelibrary.com/ruby-bridges

THE LEGACY OF RUBY BRIDGES

Ruby Bridges was just a child when she integrated William Frantz Elementary. She had not understood then the significance of her enrollment at the school. But over time, she came to understand the role she played in the civil rights movement. Today, Bridges is an activist. She gives back to her community. She started an after-school arts program at William Frantz Elementary. She founded the Ruby Bridges Foundation. The foundation uses community service projects to educate people about other cultures. Bridges has toured the country and given speeches

Ruby Bridges, *right*, poses with her former first-grade teacher, Barbara Henry, *left*, in 1998.

with her former teacher, Barbara Henry. They discussed ways to fight racism.

Bridges wrote a book about her childhood experiences in 1999. Her story continues to inspire activists today. But despite their accomplishments, there is still much work to do.

NEW ORLEANS PUBLIC SCHOOLS

Today, most white students in New Orleans do not attend public schools. They attend suburban schools or private schools in the city. Black people make up 60 percent of the city's population. They make up 85 percent of the city's public school students.

SEGREGATION'S LEGACY

Many US schools today remain segregated. But minority populations continue to grow in the United States. These population changes may be enough to force mostly white schools to integrate. Today, white families are also moving to cities in large numbers. The student makeup of public schools in cities may change as a result.

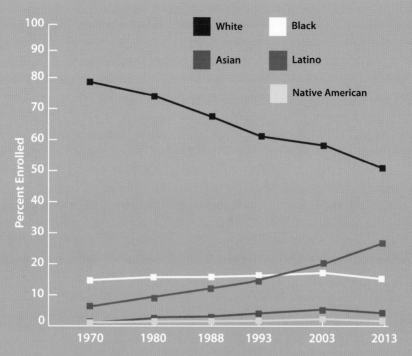

PUBLIC SCHOOL ENROLLMENT

Legend:
- White
- Black
- Asian
- Latino
- Native American

Y-axis: Percent Enrolled (0–100)

X-axis: 1970, 1980, 1988, 1993, 2003, 2013

The above graph shows the racial makeup of US public schools from 1970 to 2013. What trends do you notice? What do you think may be the reasons for these trends? How do you think this may change in the future?

Public policy can also help the process of desegregation by reducing housing segregation. Majority-white suburbs often create their own majority-white school districts. In this way, housing segregation leads to school segregation. Some cities have made efforts to reduce housing segregation. Officials made housing available to people at different income levels. Activists hope that these methods can be applied across the country.

The fight to desegregate schools continues. Activists and schoolchildren such as Bridges helped pave the way for today's desegregation efforts. Today, Norman Rockwell's painting of Bridges can be found in the Norman Rockwell Museum in Stockbridge, Massachusetts. It symbolizes the courage that children such as Ruby showed in integrating white schools.

STRAIGHT TO THE
SOURCE

In a 2010 interview, Ruby Bridges talked about the lessons she learned from her childhood experiences. She said,

I always say the lesson that I took away is the same lesson Dr. [Martin Luther King Jr.] tried to teach us before he was taken away from us: you absolutely cannot judge a person by the color of their skin. You have to allow yourself an opportunity to get to know them. And racism is something that we, as adults, have kept alive. We pass it on to our kids. None of our kids come into the world knowing anything about disliking one another. And that's the wisdom that I took away from that experience, and that is the wisdom that I pass on to kids across the country.

Source: "Wisdom from a Trailblazer: Ruby Bridges Talks Racism in Education." *NPR*. National Public Radio, December 1, 2010. Web. Accessed August 13, 2018.

Back It Up

The author of this passage is using evidence to support a point. Write a paragraph describing the point the author is making. Then write down two or three pieces of evidence the author uses to make the point.

FAST FACTS

- Throughout much of the 1900s, Jim Crow laws segregated black and white people in the South. Black and white students were forced to attend separate schools.

- The US Supreme Court ended school segregation with its ruling in *Brown v. Board of Education* in 1954. Black students faced down angry mobs and death threats when trying to integrate white schools.

- Six-year-old Ruby Bridges integrated William Frantz Elementary School in New Orleans, Louisiana, on November 14, 1960. She was one of the first African American students to integrate an elementary school in the South.

- Today, the US school system is still mostly segregated.

- Civil rights activists today fight against school segregation. They aim to achieve equal educational opportunities for African American students.

STOP AND
THINK

Say What?

Studying civil rights history can mean learning a lot of new vocabulary. Find five words in this book you've never read before. Use a dictionary to find out what they mean. Then write the meanings in your own words, and use each word in a new sentence.

Why Do I Care?

Although many US schools were integrated in the 1950s and 1960s, the legacy of segregation continues today. How do you think your life or the lives of your friends might be different without this legacy?

Surprise Me

After reading this book, what two or three facts about Ruby Bridges and the desegregation of US schools surprised you the most? Write two or three sentences about each fact. Why did you find each fact surprising?

GLOSSARY

boycott
an organized refusal to use products or services as a form of protest

desegregation
a series of government policies intended to overturn segregation

discrimination
the unjust treatment of a person or group based on race or other perceived differences

income
money that a person earns from employment

prejudice
a dislike for a group of people due to a certain characteristic, such as their race

segregated
separated from others, often because of race, religion, or gender

suburb
a small town near a larger city

white flight
the large-scale movement of white families from cities to suburbs

ONLINE
RESOURCES

To learn more about Ruby Bridges and the desegregation of US schools, visit our free resource websites below.

Visit **abdocorelibrary.com** for free Common Core resources for teachers and students, including vetted activities, multimedia, and booklinks, for deeper subject comprehension.

Visit **abdobooklinks.com** for free additional online weblinks for further learning. These links are routinely monitored and updated to provide the most current information available.

LEARN
MORE

Mooney, Carla. *The Little Rock Nine*. Minneapolis, MN: Abdo Publishing, 2016.

Wilson, Sharon J. *Brown v. Board of Education of Topeka*. Minneapolis, MN: Abdo Publishing, 2016.

ABOUT THE
AUTHORS

Duchess Harris, JD, PhD

Professor Harris is the chair of the American Studies department at Macalester College and curator of the Duchess Harris Collection of ABDO books. She is the author and coauthor of recently released ABDO books including *Hidden Human Computers: The Black Women of NASA*, *Black Lives Matter*, and *Race and Policing*.

Before working with ABDO, she authored several other books on the topics of race, culture, and American history. She served as an associate editor for *Litigation News*, the American Bar Association Section of Litigation's quarterly flagship publication, and was the first editor in chief of *Law Raza*, an interactive online journal covering race and the law, published at William Mitchell College of Law. She has earned a PhD in American Studies from the University of Minnesota and a JD from William Mitchell College of Law.

Tom Head

Tom Head is the author or coauthor of more than 30 nonfiction books, including *World History 101* and *Civil Liberties: A Beginner's Guide*. He holds a PhD in religion and society from Edith Cowan University and is a lifelong resident of Jackson, Mississippi.

INDEX